The
DHAMMAPADA

The
DHAMMAPADA

The Sayings of the Buddha

Translated by

THOMAS BYROM

Preface by Ram Dass

RIDER

LONDON • SYDNEY • AUCKLAND • JOHANNESBURG

First published in the UK in 2002 by Rider, an imprint of
Ebury Publishing
This edition published by Rider in 2008
Originally published in the USA in a different
form by Alfred A. Knopf, a division of
Random House, Inc., in 1976

Ebury Publishing is a Random House Group company

The Random House Group Limited Reg. No. 954009

Addresses for companies within the Random House Group
can be found at www.rbooks.co.uk

A CIP catalogue record for this book is available
from the British Library

Penguin Random House is committed to a sustainable future for
our business, our readers and our planet. This book is made from
Forest Stewardship Council® certified paper.

Printed and bound in Great Britain by Clays Ltd, Elcograf S.p.A.

Design by Barbara Sturman

ISBN 9781846041440

Copies are available at special rates for bulk orders. Contact the sales
development team on 020 7840 8487 for more information.

CONTENTS

8

I WISH TO RECORD my indebtedness to the translations of Müller, Gray, Wagiswara and Saunders, Woodward, Bhagwat, "J.A.," Buddhadatta Mahathera, Mascaro, and Radhakrishnan. I wish also to thank Dr. R. F. Gombrich, Reader in Pali at Oxford, for scholarly guidance; David Jarrett, Mary Jarrett, and Toinette Lippe for making my text sharper, harder, and clearer; and all the friends along the road, in Puttaparthi, Oxford, and New York, who have given me their help.

THOMAS BYROM

A C K N O W L E D G M E N T S

HERE ARE THE SAYINGS of the Buddha, the Enlightened One. Had you but ears to hear, these very words could awaken you and through them you could realize your Buddha nature. These words come to you in purity; for them to touch you they must be received in purity. These words come out of divine simplicity; to liberate you they must be heard in simplicity. These words come from the soul; to feed that in you which thirsts, these words, which are words of wisdom, not knowledge, must be heard by the soul, not the intellect. For that which feeds only the intellect entraps, while that which feeds the soul liberates. And it is the soul that thirsts for truth. The intellect thirsts only to satiate its fascination.

A transmission of truth is poured from one vessel into another. If you as a vessel are impure in body, heart, or mind, the truth cannot be contained ... what is pure becomes impure ... the power of the truth is too much ... the cup is smashed ... the transmission lost, and man continues to walk in darkness. In your lifetime you have read thousands of words such as those contained in this volume: the words of the Christ, of Lao Tsu, of the Patriarchs of Zen, of Rumi or Kabir or Saint Teresa or John, of Solomon and Abraham, of Mohammed, of Krishna or the Vedic Rishis ... words that bespeak the secrets of the Universe. But how few you have received, how many transmissions you have lost again and again because you were not ready to hear.

Is it sufficient preparation, having purchased this book, to sit in a comfortable chair, to make your reading light ready, and then to peruse this volume as you would a weekly magazine or novel, or perhaps slightly more slowly as though it were a book of poetry? Is that the way you prepare to hear the word of the Buddha, of the Christ, of Lao Tsu? Is that the way you prepare yourself to sit before a holy man and receive that jewel which could possibly liberate you from thousands of life-times on the wheel of birth and death? Were you going to meet the Buddha, might you not bathe in the river to make your body clean? Might you not come bearing a gift of a fruit or a coconut? Might you not sit with the wind and the trees and the heavens until your mind is calm? Might you not acknowledge the suffering of your fellow beings with an open heart and give alms? Might you not come forward and bow deeply in humility and sur-render? Would these not be suitable preparations for receiving the greatest truths? And when you heard the words, would you not set aside judging and allow the words to caress your being . . . to play with your consciousness as a gentle stream plays with your body, its healing waters washing away the tensions created by your models of who you are and how you think it is?

Imagine the Buddha were on earth at this moment somewhere in India. And you set out on a pilgrimage to receive a teaching from him. Perhaps you might arrive at a village such as Sarnath, where rumor has it that the Buddha is discoursing daily in the Deer Park to the gathered monks. But there they say, "No, it is too late in the season. The Buddha has gone north to the mountains." And so you set out, sometimes traveling by ox cart, more often on foot, day after day, week after week . . . from village to village, asking at each tea stop for news of the Buddha.

"Yes, he was here but a week ago. He has gone toward the east." "Yes, he was here but five days ago. He went toward the village in the north." A word here, a gesture there . . . and you know you are getting closer. Excitement of anticipating the meeting becomes all but unbearable ecstasy. As you get closer, you can tell from the light in the eyes and faces of the people that you meet that they have tasted the nectar of *darshan* (meeting) with the Buddha. Each wants to tell you of his or her experience, of the Grace: of how he walked, what he said, how he smiled. You are reminded of the Gopis who sought Krishna and said of the creeper, "Krishna has certainly been here, for see how this creeper bears the shiver of delight in its blossoms." As you get closer, the joy in anything other than meeting the Buddha becomes pale. You are single-minded in your determination. Even food and rest bow before your impatience to proceed. And finally you come to the spot on the path where the women in shawls who tend the sheep point and say, "Yes, he is up on that hill." Quickly you bathe, and then with your offering in hand you rush up the hill, stumbling over rocks and shrubs . . . but you care not for your feet because you are about to see the Holy Man. The landscape has taken on an unnatural radiance. Your body shakes; your breath comes fast. And there under a tree sits the Buddha, perfect tranquillity. You do *dundapranam,* stretching out completely before him, three times . . . and then you offer your gift of fruit for the teachings. With the slightest nod of his head, the Buddha motions for you to sit before him. You have been accepted. Never before have you felt such peace. Seated with the Buddha you are out of time, out of space. You feel only the moment . . . the breeze upon your cheek, the dog barking in the distance. It is as if the world has stopped.

After some time the Buddha speaks:

"We are what we think.
  All that we are arises with our thoughts.
  With our thoughts we make the world."

He continues to speak a few more words. Each
word burns into your soul, for these are your keys
to liberation. These words are both the goal of one
journey and the beginning of the next . . .

  After more silence he motions for you to leave.
Again you bow and go your way. By how many
campfires, by how many streams, in how many
meditation rooms will each of his words feed you
anew? Precious words so dearly obtained. But
more than the words . . . the boundless space, the
simplicity, the compassion, the peace from which
the words spring. In your hand you hold a book of
the sayings of the Buddha. Read them slowly . . .
a phrase at a time. Let them feed your soul. I wish
you the purity of body, mind, and heart to hear
them.

RAM DASS

THE DHAMMAPADA is a collection of the sayings of the Buddha (563–483 B.C.). They were probably first gathered in northern India in the third century before Christ, and originally written down in Ceylon (Sri Lanka) in the first century before Christ. *Dhamma* means law, justice, righteousness, discipline, truth; *pada* means path, step, foot, foundation. *The Dhammapada* was transmitted and recorded in Pali, the canonical language of southern Buddhism, and it has become the principal scripture for Buddhists in Sri Lanka and Southeast Asia.

The

DHAMMAPADA

1

CHOICES

We are what we think.
All that we are arises with our thoughts.
With our thoughts we make the world.
Speak or act with an impure mind
And trouble will follow you
As the wheel follows the ox that draws the cart.

We are what we think.
All that we are arises with our thoughts.
With our thoughts we make the world.
Speak or act with a pure mind
And happiness will follow you
As your shadow, unshakable.

"Look how he abused me and beat me,
  How he threw me down and robbed me."
  Live with such thoughts and you live in hate.

"Look how he abused me and beat me,
  How he threw me down and robbed me."
  Abandon such thoughts, and live in love.

In this world
Hate never yet dispelled hate.
Only love dispels hate.
This is the law,
Ancient and inexhaustible.

You too shall pass away.
Knowing this, how can you quarrel?

How easily the wind overturns a frail tree.
Seek happiness in the senses,
Indulge in food and sleep,
And you too will be uprooted.

The wind cannot overturn a mountain.
Temptation cannot touch the man
Who is awake, strong and humble,
Who masters himself and minds the law.

If a man's thoughts are muddy,
If he is reckless and full of deceit,
How can he wear the yellow robe?

Whoever is master of his own nature,
Bright, clear and true,
He may indeed wear the yellow robe.

Mistaking the false for the true
And the true for the false,
You overlook the heart
And fill yourself with desire.

See the false as false,
The true as true.
Look into your heart.
Follow your nature.

An unreflecting mind is a poor roof.
Passion, like the rain, floods the house.
But if the roof is strong, there is shelter.

Whoever follows impure thoughts
Suffers in this world and the next.
In both worlds he suffers
And how greatly
When he sees the wrong he has done.

But whoever follows the law
Is joyful here and joyful there.
In both worlds he rejoices
And how greatly
When he sees the good he has done.

For great is the harvest in this world,
And greater still in the next.

However many holy words you read,
However many you speak,
What good will they do you
If you do not act upon them?

Are you a shepherd
Who counts another man's sheep,
Never sharing the way?

Read as few words as you like
And speak fewer.
But act upon the law.

Give up the old ways—
Passion, enmity, folly.
Know the truth and find peace.
Share the way.

2

WAKEFULNESS

Wakefulness is the way to life.
The fool sleeps
As if he were already dead,
But the master is awake
And he lives forever.

He watches.
He is clear.

How happy he is!
For he sees that wakefulness is life.
How happy he is,
Following the path of the awakened.

With great perseverance
He meditates, seeking
Freedom and happiness.

So awake, reflect, watch.
Work with care and attention.
Live in the way
And the light will grow in you.

By watching and working
The master makes for himself an island
Which the flood cannot overwhelm.

The fool is careless.
But the master guards his watching.
It is his most precious treasure.

He never gives in to desire.
He meditates.
And in the strength of his resolve
He discovers true happiness.

He overcomes desire—
And from the tower of wisdom
He looks down with dispassion
Upon the sorrowing crowd.
From the mountaintop
He looks down on those
Who live close to the ground.

Mindful among the mindless,
Awake while others dream,
Swift as the race horse
He outstrips the field.

By watching
Indra became king of the gods.
How wonderful it is to watch,
How foolish to sleep.

The beggar who guards his mind
And fears the waywardness of his thoughts
Burns through every bond
With the fire of his vigilance.

The beggar who guards his mind
And fears his own confusion
Cannot fall.
He has found the way to peace.

3

MIND

As the fletcher whittles
And makes straight his arrows,
So the master directs
His straying thoughts.

Like a fish out of water,
Stranded on the shore,
Thoughts thrash and quiver.
For how can they shake off desire?

They tremble, they are unsteady,
They wander at their will.
It is good to control them,
And to master them brings happiness.

But how subtle they are,
How elusive!
The task is to quieten them,
And by ruling them to find happiness.

With single-mindedness
The master quells his thoughts.
He ends their wandering.
Seated in the cave of the heart,
He finds freedom.

How can a troubled mind
Understand the way?
If a man is disturbed
He will never be filled with knowledge.

An untroubled mind,
No longer seeking to consider
What is right and what is wrong,
A mind beyond judgments,
Watches and understands.

Know that the body is a fragile jar,
And make a castle of your mind.
In every trial
Let understanding fight for you
To defend what you have won.

For soon the body is discarded.
Then what does it feel?
A useless log of wood, it lies on the ground.
Then what does it know?

Your worst enemy cannot harm you
As much as your own thoughts, unguarded.

But once mastered,
No one can help you as much,
Not even your father or your mother.

4

FLOWERS

Who shall conquer this world
And the world of death with all its gods?
Who shall discover
The shining way of the law?

You shall, even as the man
Who seeks flowers
Finds the most beautiful,
The rarest.

34

Understand that the body
Is merely the foam of a wave,
The shadow of a shadow.
Snap the flower arrows of desire
And then, unseen,
Escape the king of death.

And travel on.

Death overtakes the man
Who gathers flowers
When with distracted mind and thirsty senses
He searches vainly for happiness
In the pleasures of the world.
Death fetches him away
As a flood carries off a sleeping village.

Death overcomes him
When with distracted mind and thirsty senses
He gathers flowers.
He will never have his fill
Of the pleasures of the world.

The bee gathers nectar from the flower
Without marring its beauty or perfume.
So let the master settle, and wander.

Look to your own faults,
What you have done or left undone.
Overlook the faults of others.

Like a lovely flower,
Bright but scentless,
Are the fine but empty words
Of the man who does not mean what he says.

Like a lovely flower,
Bright and fragrant,
Are the fine and truthful words
Of the man who means what he says.

Like garlands woven from a heap of flowers,
Fashion from your life as many good deeds.

The perfume of sandalwood,
Rosebay or jasmine
Cannot travel against the wind.

But the fragrance of virtue
Travels even against the wind,
As far as the ends of the world.

How much finer
Is the fragrance of virtue
Than of sandalwood, rosebay,
Of the blue lotus or jasmine!

The fragrance of sandalwood and rosebay
Does not travel far.
But the fragrance of virtue
Rises to the heavens.

Desire never crosses the path
Of virtuous and wakeful men.
Their brightness sets them free.

How sweetly the lotus grows
In the litter of the wayside.
Its pure fragrance delights the heart.

Follow the awakened
And from among the blind
The light of your wisdom
Will shine out, purely.

5

THE FOOL

How long the night to the watchman,
How long the road to the weary traveler,
How long the wandering of many lives
To the fool who misses the way.

If the traveler cannot find
Master or friend to go with him,
Let him travel on alone
Rather than with a fool for company.

"My children, my wealth!"
So the fool troubles himself.
But how has he children or wealth?
He is not even his own master.

The fool who knows he is a fool
Is that much wiser.
The fool who thinks he is wise
Is a fool indeed.

Does the spoon taste the soup?
A fool may live all his life
In the company of a master
And still miss the way.

The tongue tastes the soup.
If you are awake in the presence of a master
One moment will show you the way.

The fool is his own enemy.
The mischief he does is his undoing.
How bitterly he suffers!

Why do what you will regret?
Why bring tears upon yourself?

Do only what you do not regret,
And fill yourself with joy.

For a while the fool's mischief
Tastes sweet, sweet as honey.
But in the end it turns bitter.
And how bitterly he suffers!

For months the fool may fast,
Eating from the tip of a grass blade.
Still he is not worth a penny
Beside the master whose food is the way.

Fresh milk takes time to sour.
So a fool's mischief
Takes time to catch up with him.
Like the embers of a fire
It smolders within him.

Whatever a fool learns,
It only makes him duller.
Knowledge cleaves his head.

For then he wants recognition,
A place before other people,
A place over other people.

"Let them know my work,
Let everyone look to me for direction."
Such are his desires,
Such is his swelling pride.

One way leads to wealth and fame,
The other to the end of the way.

Look not for recognition
But follow the awakened
And set yourself free.

6

THE WISE MAN

The wise man tells you
Where you have fallen
And where you yet may fall—
Invaluable secrets!
Follow him, follow the way.

Let him chasten and teach you
And keep you from mischief.
The world may hate him.
But good men love him.

Do not look for bad company
Or live with men who do not care.
Find friends who love the truth.

Drink deeply.
Live in serenity and joy.
The wise man delights in the truth
And follows the law of the awakened.

The farmer channels water to his land.
The fletcher whittles his arrows.
And the carpenter turns his wood.
So the wise man directs his mind.

The wind cannot shake a mountain.
Neither praise nor blame moves the wise man.

He is clarity.
Hearing the truth,
He is like a lake,
Pure and tranquil and deep.

Want nothing.
Where there is desire,
Say nothing.

Happiness or sorrow—
Whatever befalls you,
Walk on
Untouched, unattached.

Do not ask for family or power or wealth,
Either for yourself or for another.
Can a wise man wish to rise unjustly?

Few cross over the river.
Most are stranded on this side.
On the riverbank they run up and down.

But the wise man, following the way,
Crosses over, beyond the reach of death.

He leaves the dark way
For the way of light.
He leaves his home, seeking
Happiness on the hard road.

Free from desire,
Free from possessions,
Free from the dark places of the heart.

44　　　Free from attachment and appetite,
　　　　Following the seven lights of awakening,
　　　　And rejoicing greatly in his freedom,
　　　　In this world the wise man
　　　　Becomes himself a light,
　　　　Pure, shining, free.

7

THE MASTER

At the end of the way
The master finds freedom
From desire and sorrow—
Freedom without bounds.

Those who awaken
Never rest in one place.
Like swans, they rise
And leave the lake.

On the air they rise
And fly an invisible course,
Gathering nothing, storing nothing.
Their food is knowledge.
They live upon emptiness.
They have seen how to break free.

Who can follow them?
Only the master,
Such is his purity.

Like a bird,
He rises on the limitless air
And flies an invisible course.
He wishes for nothing.
His food is knowledge.
He lives upon emptiness.
He has broken free.

He is the charioteer.
He has tamed his horses,
Pride and the senses.
Even the gods admire him.

Yielding like the earth,
Joyous and clear like the lake,
Still as the stone at the door,
He is free from life and death.

His thoughts are still.
His words are still.
His work is stillness.
He sees his freedom and is free.

The master surrenders his beliefs.
He sees beyond the end and the beginning.

He cuts all ties.
He gives up all his desires.
He resists all temptations.
And he rises.

And wherever he lives,
In the city or the country,
In the valley or in the hills,
There is great joy.

Even in the empty forest
He finds joy
Because he wants nothing.

8

THE THOUSANDS

Better than a thousand hollow words
Is one word that brings peace.

Better than a thousand hollow verses
Is one verse that brings peace.

Better than a hundred hollow lines
Is one line of the law, bringing peace.

It is better to conquer yourself
Than to win a thousand battles.

Then the victory is yours.

It cannot be taken from you,
Not by angels or by demons,
Heaven or hell.

Better than a hundred years of worship,
Better than a thousand offerings,
Better than giving up a thousand worldly ways
In order to win merit,
Better even than tending in the forest
A sacred flame for a hundred years—
Is one moment's reverence
For the man who has conquered himself.

To revere such a man,
A master old in virtue and holiness,
Is to have victory over life itself,
And beauty, strength, and happiness.

Better than a hundred years of mischief
Is one day spent in contemplation.

Better than a hundred years of ignorance
Is one day spent in reflection.

Better than a hundred years of idleness
Is one day spent in determination.

Better to live one day
Wondering
How all things arise and pass away.

Better to live one hour
Seeing
The one life beyond the way.

Better to live one moment
In the moment
Of the way beyond the way.

9

MISCHIEF

Be quick to do good.
If you are slow,
The mind, delighting in mischief,
Will catch you.

Turn away from mischief.
Again and again, turn away,
Before sorrow befalls you.

Set your heart on doing good.
Do it over and over again,
And you will be filled with joy.

A fool is happy
Until his mischief turns against him.
And a good man may suffer
Until his goodness flowers.

Do not make light of your failings,
Saying, "What are they to me?"
A jug fills drop by drop.
So the fool becomes brimful of folly.

Do not belittle your virtues,
Saying, "They are nothing."
A jug fills drop by drop.
So the wise man becomes brimful of virtue.

As the rich merchant with few servants
Shuns a dangerous road
And the man who loves life shuns poison,
Beware the dangers of folly and mischief.

For an unwounded hand may handle poison.
The innocent come to no harm.

But as dust thrown against the wind,
Mischief is blown back in the face
Of the fool who wrongs the pure and harmless.

Some are reborn in hell,
Some in this world,
The good in heaven.
But the pure are not reborn.

Nowhere!
Not in the sky,
Nor in the midst of the sea,
Nor deep in the mountains,
Can you hide from your own mischief.

Not in the sky,
Nor in the midst of the ocean,
Nor deep in the mountains,
Nowhere
Can you hide from your own death.

10

VIOLENCE

All beings tremble before violence.
All fear death.
All love life.

See yourself in others.
Then whom can you hurt?
What harm can you do?

He who seeks happiness
By hurting those who seek happiness
Will never find happiness.

For your brother is like you.
He wants to be happy.
Never harm him
And when you leave this life
You too will find happiness.

Never speak harsh words
For they will rebound upon you.
Angry words hurt
And the hurt rebounds.

Like a broken gong
Be still, be silent.
Know the stillness of freedom
Where there is no more striving.

Like herdsmen driving their cows into the field
Old age and death will drive you before them.

But the fool in his mischief forgets
And he lights the fire
Wherein one day he must burn.

He who harms the harmless
Or hurts the innocent,
Ten times shall he fall—

Into torment or infirmity,
Injury or disease or madness,
Persecution or fearful accusation,
Loss of family, loss of fortune.

Fire from heaven shall strike his house
And when his body has been struck down,
He shall rise in hell.

He who goes naked,
With matted hair, mud-bespattered,
Who fasts and sleeps on the ground
And smears his body with ashes
And sits in endless meditation—
So long as he is not free from doubts,
He will not find freedom.

58   But he who lives purely and self-assured,
        In quietness and virtue,
        Who is without harm or hurt or blame,
        Even if he wears fine clothes,
        So long as he also has faith,
        He is a true seeker.

        A noble horse rarely
        Feels the touch of the whip.
        Who is there in this world as blameless?

        Then like a noble horse
        Smart under the whip.
        Burn and be swift.

        Believe, meditate, see.
        Be harmless, be blameless.
        Awake to the law.
        And from all sorrow free yourself.

The farmer channels water to his land.
The fletcher whittles his arrows.
The carpenter turns his wood.
And the wise man masters himself.

11

OLD AGE

The world is on fire!
And are you laughing?
You are deep in the dark.
Will you not ask for light?

For behold your body—
A painted puppet, a toy,
Jointed and sick and full of false imaginings,
A shadow that shifts and fades.

How frail it is!
Frail and pestilent,
It sickens, festers, and dies.
Like every living thing
In the end it sickens and dies.

Behold these whitened bones,
The hollow shells and husks of a dying summer.
And are you laughing?

You are a house of bones,
Flesh and blood for plaster.
Pride lives in you,
And hypocrisy, decay, and death.

The glorious chariots of kings shatter.
So also the body turns to dust.
But the spirit of purity is changeless
And so the pure instruct the pure.

The ignorant man is an ox.
He grows in size, not in wisdom.

"Vainly I sought the builder of my house
Through countless lives.
I could not find him . . .
How hard it is to tread life after life!

"But now I see you, O builder!
And never again shall you build my house.
I have snapped the rafters,
Split the ridgepole
And beaten out desire.
And now my mind is free."

There are no fish in the lake.
The long-legged cranes stand in the water.

Sad is the man who in his youth
Lived loosely and squandered his fortune—

Sad as a broken bow,
And sadly is he sighing
After all that has arisen and has passed away.

12

YOURSELF

Love yourself and watch—
Today, tomorrow, always.

First establish yourself in the way,
Then teach,
And so defeat sorrow.

To straighten the crooked
You must first do a harder thing—
Straighten yourself.

64   You are your only master.
      Who else?
      Subdue yourself,
      And discover your master.

      Willfully you have fed
      Your own mischief.
      Soon it will crush you
      As the diamond crushes stone.

      By your own folly
      You will be brought as low
      As your worst enemy wishes.
      So the creeper chokes the tree.

      How hard it is to serve yourself,
      How easy to lose yourself
      In mischief and folly.

      The *kashta* reed dies when it bears fruit.
      So the fool,
      Scorning the teachings of the awakened,
      Spurning those who follow the law,
      Perishes when his folly flowers.

Mischief is yours.
Sorrow is yours.
But virtue also is yours,
And purity.

You are the source
Of all purity and all impurity.

No one purifies another.

Never neglect your work
For another's,
However great his need.

Your work is to discover your work
And then with all your heart
To give yourself to it.

13

THE WORLD

Do not live in the world,
In distraction and false dreams,
Outside the law.

Arise and watch.
Follow the way joyfully
Through this world and beyond.

Follow the way of virtue.
Follow the way joyfully
Through this world and on beyond!

For consider the world—
A bubble, a mirage.
See the world as it is,
And death shall overlook you.

Come, consider the world,
A painted chariot for kings,
A trap for fools.
But he who sees goes free.

As the moon slips from behind a cloud
And shines,
So the master comes out from behind his
    ignorance
And shines.

This world is in darkness.
How few have eyes to see!
How few the birds
Who escape the net and fly to heaven!

Swans rise and fly toward the sun.
What magic!
So do the pure conquer the armies of illusion
And rise and fly.

If you scoff at heaven
And violate the law,
If your words are lies,
Where will your mischief end?

The fool laughs at generosity.
The miser cannot enter heaven.
But the master finds joy in giving
And happiness is his reward.

And more—
For greater than all the joys
Of heaven and earth,
Greater still than dominion
Over all the worlds,
Is the joy of reaching the stream.

14

THE MAN WHO IS AWAKE

He is awake.
The victory is his.
He has conquered the world.

How can he lose the way
Who is beyond the way?
His eye is open.
His foot is free.
Who can follow after him?

The world cannot reclaim him
Or lead him astray,
Nor can the poisoned net of desire hold him.

He is awake!
The gods watch over him.

He is awake
And finds joy in the stillness of meditation
And in the sweetness of surrender.

Hard it is to be born,
Hard it is to live,
Harder still to hear of the way,
And hard to rise, follow, and awake.

Yet the teaching is simple.
Do what is right.
Be pure.
At the end of the way is freedom.
Till then, patience.

If you wound or grieve another,
You have not learned detachment.

Offend in neither word nor deed.
Eat with moderation.
Live in your heart.
Seek the highest consciousness.

Master yourself according to the law.
This is the simple teaching of the awakened.

The rain could turn to gold
And still your thirst would not be slaked.
Desire is unquenchable
Or it ends in tears, even in heaven.

He who wishes to awake
Consumes his desires
Joyfully.

In his fear a man may shelter
In mountains or in forests,
In groves of sacred trees or in shrines.
But how can he hide there from his sorrow?

He who shelters in the way
And travels with those who follow it
Comes to see the four great truths.

Concerning sorrow,
The beginning of sorrow,
The eightfold way,
And the end of sorrow.

Then at last he is safe.
He has shaken off sorrow.
He is free.

The awakened are few and hard to find.
Happy is the house where a man awakes.

Blessed is his birth.
Blessed is the teaching of the way.
Blessed is the understanding among those who
    follow it,
And blessed is their determination.

And blessed are they who revere
The man who awakes and follows the way.

They are free from fear.
They are free.

They have crossed over the river of sorrow.

15

JOY

Live in joy,
In love,
Even among those who hate.

Live in joy,
In health,
Even among the afflicted.

Live in joy,
In peace,
Even among the troubled.

Live in joy,
Without possessions,
Like the shining ones.

The winner sows hatred
Because the loser suffers.
Let go of winning and losing
And find joy.

There is no fire like passion,
No crime like hatred,
No sorrow like separation,
No sickness like hunger,
And no joy like the joy of freedom.

Health, contentment, and trust
Are your greatest possessions,
And freedom your greatest joy.

Look within.
Be still.
Free from fear and attachment,
Know the sweet joy of the way.

How joyful to look upon the awakened
And to keep company with the wise.

How long the road to the man
Who travels with a fool.
But whoever follows those who follow the way
Discovers his family, and is filled with joy.

Follow then the shining ones,
The wise, the awakened, the loving,
For they know how to work and forbear.

Follow them
As the moon follows the path of the stars.

16

PLEASURE

Do not let pleasure distract you
From meditation, from the way.

Free yourself from pleasure and pain.
For in craving pleasure or in nursing pain
There is only sorrow.

Like nothing lest you lose it,
Lest it bring you grief and fear.
Go beyond likes and dislikes.

From passion and desire,
Sensuousness and lust,
Arise grief and fear.
Free yourself from attachment.

He is pure, and sees.
He speaks the truth, and lives it.
He does his own work.
So he is admired and loved.

With a determined mind and undesiring heart
He longs for freedom.
He is called *uddhamsoto*—
"He who goes upstream."

When a traveler at last comes home
From a far journey,
With what gladness
His family and his friends receive him!

Even so shall your good deeds
Welcome you like friends
And with what rejoicing
When you pass from this life to the next!

17

ANGER

Let go of anger.
Let go of pride.
When you are bound by nothing
You go beyond sorrow.

Anger is like a chariot careering wildly.
He who curbs his anger is the true charioteer.
Others merely hold the reins.

With gentleness overcome anger.
With generosity overcome meanness.
With truth overcome deceit.

Speak the truth.
Give whatever you can.
Never be angry.
These three steps will lead you
Into the presence of the gods.

The wise harm no one.
They are masters of their bodies
And they go to the boundless country.
They go beyond sorrow.

Those who seek perfection
Keep watch by day and night
Till all desires vanish.

Listen, Atula. This is not new,
It is an old saying—
They blame you for being silent,
They blame you when you talk too much
And when you talk too little."
Whatever you do, they blame you.

The world always finds
A way to praise and a way to blame.
It always has and it always will.

But who dares blame the man
Whom the wise continually praise,
Whose life is virtuous and wise,
Who shines like a coin of pure gold?

Even the gods praise him.
Even Brahma praises him.

Beware of the anger of the body.
Master the body.
Let it serve truth.

Beware of the anger of the mouth.
Master your words.
Let them serve truth.

Beware of the anger of the mind.
Master your thoughts.
Let them serve truth.

The wise have mastered
Body, word, and mind.

They are the true masters.

18

IMPURITY

You are as the yellow leaf.
The messengers of death are at hand.
You are to travel far away.
What will you take with you?

You are the lamp
To lighten the way.
Then hurry, hurry.

When your light shines
Without impurity or desire
You will come into the boundless country.

Your life is falling away.
Death is at hand.
Where will you rest on the way?
What have you taken with you?

You are the lamp
To lighten the way.
Then hurry, hurry.

When your light shines purely
You will not be born
And you will not die.

As a silversmith sifts dust from silver,
Remove your own impurities
Little by little.

Or as iron is corroded by rust
Your own mischief will consume you.

Neglected, the sacred verses rust.
For beauty rusts without use
And unrepaired the house falls into ruin,
And the watch, without vigilance, fails.

In this world and the next
There is impurity and impurity:
When a woman lacks dignity,
When a man lacks generosity.

But the greatest impurity is ignorance.
Free yourself from it.
Be pure.

Life is easy
For the man who is without shame,
Impudent as a crow,
A vicious gossip,
Vain, meddlesome, dissolute.

But life is hard
For the man who quietly undertakes
The way of perfection,
With purity, detachment, and vigor.
He sees light.

If you kill, lie, or steal,
Commit adultery, or drink,
You dig up your own roots.

And if you cannot master yourself,
The harm you do turns against you
Grievously.

You may give in the spirit of light
Or as you please,
But if you care how another man gives
Or how he withholds,
You trouble your quietness endlessly.

These envying roots!
Destroy them
And enjoy a lasting quietness.

There is no fire like passion,
There are no chains like hate.
Illusion is a net,
Desire a rushing river.

How easy it is to see your brother's faults,
How hard to face your own.
You winnow his in the wind like chaff,
But yours you hide,
Like a cheat covering up an unlucky throw.

Dwelling on your brother's faults
Multiplies your own.
You are far from the end of your journey.

The way is not in the sky.
The way is in the heart.

See how you love
Whatever keeps you from your journey.

But the *tathagathas*,
"They who have gone beyond,"
Have conquered the world.
They are free.

The way is not in the sky.
The way is in the heart.

All things arise and pass away.
But the awakened awake forever.

19

THE JUST

If you determine your course
With force or speed,
You miss the way of the law.

Quietly consider
What is right and what is wrong.
Receiving all opinions equally,
Without haste, wisely,
Observe the law.

Who is wise,
The eloquent or the quiet man?
Be quiet,
And loving and fearless.

For the mind talks.
But the body knows.

Gray hairs do not make a master.
A man may grow old in vain.

The true master lives in truth,
In goodness and restraint,
Nonviolence, moderation, and purity.

Fine words or fine features
Cannot make a master
Out of a jealous and greedy man.

Only when envy and selfishness
Are rooted out of him
May he grow in beauty.

A man may shave his head
But if he still lies and neglects his work,
If he clings to desire and attachment,
How can he follow the way?

The true seeker
Subdues all waywardness.
He has submitted his nature to quietness.

He is a true seeker
Not because he begs
But because he follows the lawful way,
Holding back nothing, holding to nothing,
Beyond good and beyond evil,
Beyond the body and beyond the mind.

Silence cannot make a master out of a fool.

But he who weighs only purity in his scales,
Who sees the nature of the two worlds,
He is a master.

He harms no living thing.

And yet it is not good conduct
That helps you upon the way,
Nor ritual, nor book learning,
Nor withdrawal into the self,
Nor deep meditation.
None of these confers mastery or joy.

O seeker!
Rely on nothing
Until you want nothing.

20

THE WAY

The way is eightfold.
There are four truths.
All virtue lies in detachment.
The master has an open eye.

This is the only way,
The only way to the opening of the eye.
Follow it.
Outwit desire.

Follow it to the end of sorrow.

When I pulled out sorrow's shaft
I showed you the way.

94

It is you who must make the effort.
The masters only point the way.

But if you meditate
And follow the law
You will free yourself from desire.

"Everything arises and passes away."
When you see this, you are above sorrow.
This is the shining way.

"Existence is sorrow."
Understand, and go beyond sorrow.
This is the way of brightness.

"Existence is illusion."
Understand, go beyond.
This is the way of clarity.

You are strong, you are young.
It is time to arise.
So arise!
Lest through irresolution and idleness
You lose the way.

Master your words.
Master your thoughts.
Never allow your body to do harm.
Follow these three roads with purity
And you will find yourself upon the one way,
The way of wisdom.

Sit in the world, sit in the dark.
Sit in meditation, sit in light.
Choose your seat.
Let wisdom grow.

Cut down the forest,
Not the tree.
For out of the forest comes danger.

Cut down the forest.
Fell desire.
And set yourself free.

While a man desires a woman,
His mind is bound
As closely as a calf to its mother.

As you would pluck an autumn lily,
Pluck the arrow of desire.

For he who is awake
Has shown you the way of peace.
Give yourself to the journey.

"Here shall I make my dwelling,
In the summer and the winter,
And in the rainy season."
So the fool makes his plans,
Sparing not a thought for his death.

Death overtakes the man
Who, giddy and distracted by the world,
Cares only for his flocks and his children.
Death fetches him away
As a flood carries off a sleeping village.

His family cannot save him,
Not his father nor his sons.

Know this.
Seek wisdom, and purity.
Quickly clear the way.

21

OUT OF THE FOREST

There is pleasure
And there is bliss.
Forgo the first to possess the second.

If you are happy
At the expense of another man's happiness,
You are forever bound.

You do not what you should.
You do what you should not.
You are reckless, and desire grows.

But the master is wakeful.
He watches his body.
In all his actions he discriminates,
And he becomes pure.

He is without blame
Though once he may have murdered
His mother and his father,
Two kings, a kingdom, and all its subjects.

Though the kings were holy
And their subjects among the virtuous,
Yet is he blameless.

The followers of the awakened
Awake
And day and night they watch
And meditate upon their master.

Forever wakeful,
They mind the law.

They know their brothers on the way.

They understand the mystery of the body.

They find joy in all beings,

They delight in meditation.

It is hard to live in the world
And hard to live out of it.
It is hard to be one among many.

And for the wanderer, how long is the road
Wandering through many lives!

Let him rest.
Let him not suffer.
Let him not fall into suffering.

If he is a good man,
A man of faith, honored and prosperous,
Wherever he goes he is welcome.

Like the Himalayas
Good men shine from afar.

But bad men move unseen
Like arrows in the night.

Sit.
Rest.
Work.

Alone with yourself,
Never weary.

On the edge of the forest
Live joyfully,
Without desire.

22

THE DARK

One man denies the truth.
Another denies his own actions.
Both go into the dark
And in the next world suffer
For they offend truth.

Wear the yellow robe.
But if you are reckless
You will fall into darkness.

If you are reckless,
Better to swallow molten iron
Than eat at the table of good folk.

If you court another man's wife
You court trouble.
Your sleep is broken.
You lose your honor.
You fall into darkness.

You go against the law,
You go into the dark.
Your pleasures end in fear
And the king's punishment is harsh.

But as a blade of grass held awkwardly
May cut your hand,
So renunciation may lead you into the dark.

For if in your renunciation
You are reckless and break your word,
If your purpose wavers,
You will not find light.

Do what you have to do
Resolutely, with all your heart.
The traveler who hesitates
Only raises dust on the road.

It is better to do nothing
Than to do what is wrong.
For whatever you do, you do to yourself.

Like a border town well guarded,
Guard yourself within and without.
Let not a single moment pass
Lest you fall into darkness.

Feel shame only where shame is due.
Fear only what is fearful.
See evil only in what is evil.
Lest you mistake the true way
And fall into darkness.

See what is.
See what is not.
Follow the true way.
Rise.

23

THE ELEPHANT

I shall endure hard words
As the elephant endures the shafts of battle.
For many people speak wildly.

The tamed elephant goes to battle.
The king rides him.
The tamed man is the master.
He can endure hard words in peace.

Better than a mule
Or the fine horses of Sindh
Or mighty elephants of war
Is the man who has mastered himself.

Not on their backs
Can he reach the untrodden country,
But only on his own.

The mighty elephant Dhanapalaka
Is wild when he is in rut,
And when bound he will not eat,
Remembering the elephant grove.

The fool is idle.
He eats and he rolls in his sleep
Like a hog in a sty.
And he has to live life over again.

"My own mind used to wander
Wherever pleasure or desire or lust led it.
But now I have it tamed,
I guide it,
As the keeper guides the wild elephant."

Awake.
Be the witness of your thoughts.
The elephant hauls himself from the mud.
In the same way drag yourself out of your sloth.

If the traveler can find
A virtuous and wise companion
Let him go with him joyfully
And overcome the dangers of the way.

But if you cannot find
Friend or master to go with you,
Travel on alone—
Like a king who has given away his kingdom,
Like an elephant in the forest.

Travel on alone,
Rather than with a fool for company.

Do not carry with you your mistakes.
Do not carry your cares.

Travel on alone
Like an elephant in the forest.

To have friends in need is sweet
And to share happiness.
And to have done something good
Before leaving this life is sweet,
And to let go of sorrow.

To be a mother is sweet,
And a father.
It is sweet to live arduously,
And to master yourself.

O how sweet it is to enjoy life,
Living in honesty and strength!

And wisdom is sweet,
And freedom.

24

DESIRE

If you sleep
Desire grows in you
Like a vine in the forest.

Like a monkey in the forest
You jump from tree to tree,
Never finding the fruit—
From life to life,
Never finding peace.

If you are filled with desire
Your sorrows swell
Like the grass after the rain.

But if you subdue desire
Your sorrows fall from you
Like drops of water from a lotus flower.

This is good counsel
And it is for everyone:
As the grass is cleared for the fresh root,
Cut down desire
Lest death after death crush you
As a river crushes the helpless reeds.

For if the roots hold firm,
A felled tree grows up again.
If desires are not uprooted,
Sorrows grow again in you.

Thirty-six streams are rushing toward you!
Desire and pleasure and lust . . .
Play in your imagination with them
And they will sweep you away.

Powerful streams!
They flow everywhere.

Strong vine!
If you see it spring up,
Take care!
Pull it out by the roots.

Pleasures flow everywhere.
You float upon them
And are carried from life to life.

Like a hunted hare you run,
The pursuer of desire pursued,
Harried from life to life.

O seeker!
Give up desire.
Shake off your chains.

You have come out of the hollow
Into the clearing.
The clearing is empty.
Why do you rush back into the hollow?

112

Desire is a hollow
And people say, "Look!
He was free.
But now he gives up his freedom."

It is not iron that imprisons you
Nor rope nor wood,
But the pleasure you take in gold and jewels,
In sons and wives.

Soft fetters,
Yet they hold you down.
Can you snap them?

There are those who can,
Who surrender the world,
Forsake desire, and follow the way.

O slave of desire,
Float upon the stream.
Little spider, stick to your web.
Or else abandon your sorrows for the way.

Abandon yesterday, and tomorrow,
And today.
Cross over to the farther shore,
Beyond life and death.

Do your thoughts trouble you?
Does passion disturb you?
Beware of thirstiness
Lest your wishes become desires
And desire binds you.

Quieten your mind.
Reflect.
Watch.
Nothing binds you.
You are free.

You are strong.
You have come to the end.
Free from passion and desire,
You have stripped the thorns from the stem.
This is your last body.

You are wise.
You are free from desire
And you understand words
And the stitching together of words.
And you want nothing.

"Victory is mine,
Knowledge is mine,
And all purity,
All surrender.

"I want nothing.
I am free.
I found my way.
Whom shall I call Teacher?"

The gift of truth is beyond giving.
The taste beyond sweetness,
The joy beyond joy.

The end of desire is the end of sorrow.

The fool is his own enemy.
Seeking wealth, he destroys himself.

Seek rather the other shore.

Weeds choke the field.
Passion poisons the nature of man,
And hatred, illusion, and desire.

Honor the man who is without passion,
Hatred, illusion, and desire.

What you give to him
Will be given back to you,
And more.

25

THE SEEKER

Master your senses,
What you taste and smell,
What you see, what you hear.

In all things be a master
Of what you do and say and think.
Be free.

You are a seeker.
Delight in the mastery
Of your hands and your feet,
Of your words and your thoughts.

Delight in meditation
And in solitude.
Compose yourself, be happy.
You are a seeker.

Hold your tongue.
Do not exalt yourself
But lighten the way
For your words are sweet.

Follow the truth of the way.
Reflect upon it.
Make it your own.
Live it.
It will always sustain you.

Do not turn away what is given you,
Nor reach out for what is given to others,
Lest you disturb your quietness.

Give thanks
For what has been given you,
However little.
Be pure, never falter.

THE SEEKER

118

You have no name and no form.
Why miss what you do not have?
The seeker is not sorry.

Love and joyfully
Follow the way,
The quiet way to the happy country.

Seeker!
Empty the boat,
Lighten the load,
Passion and desire and hatred.

And sail swiftly.

There are five at the door
To turn away, and five more,
And there are five to welcome in.

And when five* have been left
Stranded on the shore,
The seeker is called *oghatinnoti*—
"He who has crossed over."

Seeker!
Do not be reckless.
Meditate constantly.
Or you will swallow fire
And cry out: "No more!"

If you are not wise,
How can you steady the mind?
If you cannot quieten yourself,
What will you ever learn?

How will you become free?

---

*The first five are selfishness, doubt, false spirituality, passion, hatred. The second five are longing for birth both with a body, and without one, vanity, mental restlessness, ignorance. The third five are faith, vigilance, energy, meditation, wisdom. The five left behind are greed, hatred, delusion, pride, false teaching.

With a quiet mind
Come into that empty house, your heart,
And feel the joy of the way
Beyond the world.

Look within—
The rising and the falling.
What happiness!
How sweet to be free!

It is the beginning of life,
Of mastery and patience,
Of good friends along the way,
Of a pure and active life.

So live in love.
Do your work.
Make an end of your sorrows.

For see how the jasmine
Releases and lets fall
Its withered flowers.

Let fall willfulness and hatred.

Are you quiet?
Quieten your body.
Quieten your mind.

You want nothing.
Your words are still.
You are still.

By your own efforts
Waken yourself, watch yourself.
And live joyfully.

You are the master,
You are the refuge.
As a merchant breaks in a fine horse,
Master yourself.

How gladly you follow
The words of the awakened.

How quietly, how surely
You approach the happy country,
The heart of stillness.

122   However young,
      The seeker who sets out upon the way
      Shines bright over the world.

      Like the moon,
      Come out from behind the clouds!
      Shine.

26

THE TRUE MASTER

Wanting nothing
With all your heart
Stop the stream.

When the world dissolves
Everything becomes clear.

Go beyond
This way or that way,
To the farther shore
Where the world dissolves
And everything becomes clear.

124

Beyond this shore
And the farther shore,
Beyond the beyond,
Where there is no beginning,
No end.

Without fear, go.

Meditate.
Live purely.
Be quiet.
Do your work, with mastery.

By day the sun shines,
And the warrior in his armor shines.
By night the moon shines,
And the master shines in meditation.

But day and night
The man who is awake
Shines in the radiance of the spirit.

A master gives up mischief.
He is serene.
He leaves everything behind him.

He does not take offense
And he does not give it.
He never returns evil for evil.

Alas for the man
Who raises his hand against another,
And even more for him
Who returns the blow.

Resist the pleasures of life
And the desire to hurt—
Till sorrows vanish.

Never offend
By what you think or say or do.

Honor the man who is awake
And shows you the way.
Honor the fire of his sacrifice.

Matted hair or family or caste
Do not make a master
But the truth and goodness
With which he is blessed.

Your hair is tangled
And you sit on a deerskin.
What folly!
When inside you are ragged with lust.

The master's clothes are in tatters.
His veins stand out,
He is wasting away.
Alone in the forest
He sits and meditates.

A man is not born to mastery.
A master is never proud.
He does not talk down to others.
Owning nothing, he misses nothing.

He is not afraid.
He does not tremble.
Nothing binds him.
He is infinitely free.

So cut through
The strap and the thong and the rope.
Loosen the fastenings.
Unbolt the doors of sleep
And awake.

The master endures
Insults and ill treatment
Without reacting.
For his spirit is an army.

He is never angry.
He keeps his promises.
He never strays, he is determined.
This body is my last, he says!

Like water on the leaf of a lotus flower
Or a mustard seed on the point of a needle,
He does not cling.

For he has reached the end of sorrow
And has laid down his burden.

He looks deeply into things
And sees their nature.
He discriminates
And reaches the end of the way.

He does not linger
With those who have a home
Nor with those who stray.
Wanting nothing,
He travels on alone.

He hurts nothing.
He never kills.

He moves with love among the unloving,
With peace and detachment
Among the hungry and querulous.

Like a mustard seed from the point of a needle
Hatred has fallen from him,
And lust, hypocrisy, and pride.

He offends no one.
Yet he speaks the truth.
His words are clear
But never harsh.

Whatever is not his
He refuses,
Good or bad, great or small.

He wants nothing from this world
And nothing from the next.
He is free.

Desiring nothing, doubting nothing,
Beyond judgment and sorrow
And the pleasures of the senses,
He has moved beyond time.
He is pure and free.

How clear he is.
He is the moon.
He is serene.
He shines.

For he has traveled
Life after life
The muddy and treacherous road of illusion.

He does not tremble
Or grasp or hesitate.
He has found peace.

Calmly
He lets go of life,
Of home and pleasure and desire.

Nothing of men can hold him.
Nothing of the gods can hold him.
Nothing in all creation can hold him.

Desire has left him,
Never to return.
Sorrow has left him,
Never to return.

He is calm.
In him the seed of renewing life
Has been consumed.
He has conquered all the inner worlds.

With dispassionate eye
He sees everywhere
The falling and the uprising.

And with great gladness
He knows that he has finished.
He has woken from his sleep.

And the way he has taken
Is hidden from men,
Even from spirits and gods,
By virtue of his purity.

In him there is no yesterday,
No tomorrow,
No today.

Possessing nothing,
Wanting nothing.

He is full of power.
Fearless, wise, exalted.
He has vanquished all things.
He sees by virtue of his purity.

He has come to the end of the way,
Over the river of his many lives,
His many deaths.

Beyond the sorrow of hell,
Beyond the great joy of heaven,
By virtue of his purity.

He has come to the end of the way.

All that he had to do, he has done.

And now he is one.

THOMAS (BILLY) BYROM, PH.D., was born in England and educated at Balliol College, Oxford, and Harvard. He taught history and literature at Harvard and Old and Middle English language and Victorian and modern literature at Oxford, where he was first a fellow of Exeter College and then a fellow in American Studies of St. Catherine's College. His translation of *The Ashtavakra Gita* was published under the title *The Heart of Awareness*.

Byrom studied with the American teacher Ma Jaya Sati Bhagavati. In 1976 he moved to Kashi Ashram in Sebastian, Florida, where he served as president of the Kashi Foundation and as a spiritual elder and counselor for the whole community. He was cofounder and director of the Ma Jaya River School and lived at Kashi until his death in 1991.

The Wise Heart
Buddhist Psychology for the West

Jack Kornfield

For over 2000 years, Buddhist psychology has offered invaluable insights into the nature of the heart and mind. Drawing on his experience as a monk, as well as an expert psychologist, Jack Kornfield provides an accessible, definitive guide for Buddhists and non-Buddhists alike, offering practical tools for coping with modern life and dealing with emotions such as fear, anger and shame.

The Tibetan Book of Living and Dying

A Spiritual Classic from One of the Foremost
Interpreters of Tibetan Buddhism to the West

Sogyal Rinpoche

This highly acclaimed book clarifies the majestic
vision of life and death that underlies the Tibetan
tradition. Including not only a lucid and complete
introduction to the practice of meditation but also
advice on how to care for the dying with love and
compassion, this classic work will inspire all who
read it to begin the journey to enlightenment and
so become 'servants of peace' working in the world.

How to See Yourself As You Really Are
A Practical Guide to Self-Knowledge

His Holiness the Dalai Lama

Based on a fundamental Buddhist notion that love and insight work together to bring about enlightenment like two wings of a bird, *How to See Yourself As You Really Are* provides a new perspective on the psychological problems of hurting ourselves through misguided, exaggerated notions of self, others, events and physical things. Drawing on wisdom and techniques refined in Tibetan monasteries for more than a thousand years His Holiness the Dalai Lama gives readers a clear path to assess their growth and progress with intimate accounts of his life-long experiences.

The Miracle of Mindfulness

The Classic Guide to Meditation by
the World's Most Revered Master

Thich Nhat Hanh

Thich Nhat Hanh's gentle anecdotes and practical
exercises help us to arrive at greater self-
understanding and peacefulness, whether we are
beginners or advanced students of mindfulness.
Irrespective of our particular religious beliefs, we
can begin to reap the immense benefits that
meditation has been scientifically proven to offer.
We can all learn to experience the miracle of
mindfulness for ourselves.

The Miracle of Mindfulness
The Art of Power
The World We Have

Thich Nhat Hanh

Thich Nhat Hanh's gentle anecdotes and practical exercises help us to arrive at greater self-understanding and acceptance. Whether we are a beginner or advanced student of meditation, Buddhist or non-Buddhist, we can all gain the many benefits that meditation has been scientifically proven to ... we can, perhaps, perhaps, the miracle of mindfulness experience.